Dad's Gift

by Judy Veramendi
illustrated by Jackie Urbanovic

Scott Foresman

Editorial Offices: Glenview, Illinois • New York, New York
Sales Offices: Reading, Massachusetts • Duluth, Georgia
Glenview, Illinois • Carrollton, Texas • Menlo Park, California

Pam had a pal.
Her pal's name was Jill.
They had fun together.

Jill had a little cat.
Jill's cat had a long tail.
The cat ran after its tail.

The cat was so cute.
It was very little.
It was just right for Jill.

Pam sighed.
"I want a cat like Jill's.
I'll play with it.
I'll play every night!"

5

One night Pam found a gift.
It was from her dad.

Pam asked, "What can it be?"
Her dad said, "Take a look!"

It was Pam's old stuffed cat.
A note was tied on its neck.
"This is not funny," said Pam.
"Read the note," said her dad.

Pam went to a bright light.
She read the note.

Pam sighed.

Pam's mom said, "Come on!
Start looking!"

First Pam looked to her left.
She did not see anything.
Her dad said, "Look to the right!"
Pam saw something black.

It was a cat!

She picked up her dad's gift.

She held the cat tight.

It was just right!

Phonics for Families: This book gives your child practice reading words with long *i* spelled *igh* and *ie,* as in *night* and *tied;* words that indicate possession, such as *Pam's;* and the high-frequency words *together, found, start,* and *first.* Read the book together. Then have your child find the story words that have long *i,* spelled *igh.*

Phonics Skills: Long *i* spelled *igh, ie;* Possessives (singular)

High-Frequency Words: *first, found, start, together*